It's the Law!
The U.S. Constitution from A to Z

by

Joseline Jean-Louis Hardrick

A project of
Twelve:Two Training, LLC

Any Book That Inspires™
A Division of Twelve:Two Training, LLC

Visit my website
www. joselinehardrick.com
and sign up for my mailing list
for free worksheets and
educational resources.

To all the children
who will inherit our democracy.
JJH

– A is for Amendment –
When it's time to make a change
and adjust the Constitution,
we make a new amendment
to avoid any confusion.

– B is for Bill of Rights –
The first ten amendments
that protect the rights of each
to express their freedom
of religion, press, and speech.

– C is for Congress –
It's the legislative branch
which means they make the laws.
They have the power to tax, spend,
and support each cause.

- D is for Declaration of Independence -
Thomas Jefferson wrote it out.
It's a list of resolutions.
The document that started it all,
including the revolution.

- E is for Equal Protection -
It's in the Fourteenth Amendment,
and it has a powerful clause!
We all get certain protections
equally under the laws.

– F is for Freedom –
We have a lot of freedom
and responsibility.
We do what makes us happy,
preserve life and liberty.

– G is for Government –
Both federal and state
are run by public officials.
They each have three branches,
executive, legislative, and judicial.

- H is for House of Representatives -
It's one-half of Congress
and chosen by population.
Each state gets a different amount
so it grows along with the nation.

- I is for Immunities and Privileges -
Benefits and protections
that we all share.
For citizens of this nation,
every state must take care.

– J is for Judicial Branch –
As in the Supreme Court
and every federal judge.
When they interpret specific laws
they usually don't like to budge.

– K is for Kings (and Queens) –
There's no more royalty.
We don't allow them here.
The Constitution bans nobility
to make it very clear.

– L is for Laws –
As in the Constitution,
and statutes, codes, and regulations.
They all make up the set of rules
we must obey throughout the nation.

– M is for Majority Rule –
The majority makes the rule.
At least that's what they say.
When more than 50% say yes (or no)
they're supposed to get their way.

– N is for Naturalization –
To become a citizen
instead of a permanent guest,
you're either born in the *U.S.*
or swear under oath and take a test.

- O is for Original Intent -
There's lots of debate
about original intent.
Even if the Founders wrote it,
how do we know what they really meant?

– P is for President –
Once Congress passes laws
The President must execute,
give pardons, write orders,
and receive the military salute.

– Q is for Qualifications –
There are many qualifications
to work for the government,
like age and citizenship,
and being a resident.

- R is for Rights -
There are many more rights
than the ones under letter "B."
You have to read between the lines
for dignity and privacy.

- S is for Senate -
The other half of Congress,
they help to make laws too.
They have a lot of power since
each state only gets two.

— T is for Taxes —
Some pay it and some don't,
but we all benefit.
Let's hope they balance it out,
and get rid of the deficit.

– U is for Union –
As a union, we stand,
and that's by design.
All the benefits and burdens
are yours and mine.

- V is for Voting -
Vote every election
for the public good.
Many fought and died so
that every citizen could.

– W is for We the People –
For *women*, *workers*, and
the *worldwide* community.
For all to participate
for the sake of our unity.

– X Marks the Spot –
That's where thirty-nine men
on the dotted line signed
to create this republic,
a new government refined.

– Y is for Yearly Celebration –
America's yearly celebration
is the Fourth of July,
when everyone comes out
to watch fireworks in the sky.

- Z is for Zealous -
Zealous protection
of our right to be free.
Fairness and justice
for all is our guarantee.

Joseline J. Hardrick

I love reading children's books. When I taught elementary school many years ago, my favorite part of the day was reading to the kids. Now that I have my own son, Little George, I have read many more books and have been inspired to write my own. My son was not impressed with the first one I wrote, so I kept trying until he laughed aloud while I read it.

So began my journey as a children's book author. And now Little George has joined me in writing some of the books; from story ideas to illustrations, we worked together to create fun stories for young kids.

I hope your child enjoys this book as much as I enjoyed making it. Please consider leaving a review on Amazon.com. Visit my website at www.joselinehardrick.com or by scanning the QR code for free activity worksheets.

www.ingramcontent.com/pod-product-compliance
Lightning Source LLC
Chambersburg PA
CBHW042010080426
42734CB00002B/38

9781958912003